AT AGE 2, JUSTIN BEGAN HIS CAREER IN MUSIC BY LEARNING TO PLAY THE DRUMS. HE THEN TURNED TO THE PIANO, AND EVENTUALLY GUITAR...

...WHICH HE PLAYED IN FRONT OF STRATFORD'S AVON THEATRE TO MAKE MONEY TO GO GOLFING WITH HIS BUDDIES.

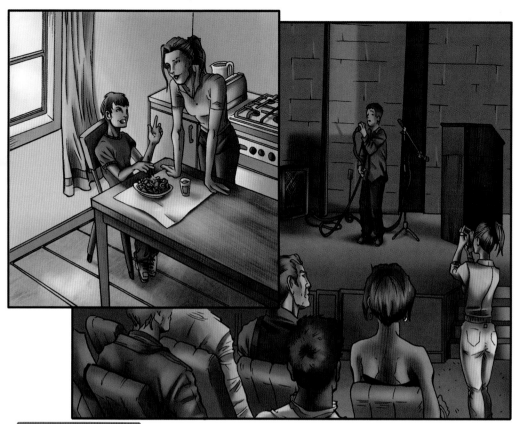

ACCORDING TO JUSTIN, "NOTHING EVER CAME OUT OF STRATFORD."

SO JUSTIN'S MOTHER DECIDED TO GO GLOBAL. SHE TOOK TO **YOU TUBE** WHERE SHE UPLOADED FOOTAGE OF HER SON PERFORMING AT A LOCAL SINGING COMPETITION. INITIALLY, THE FOOTAGE WAS MEANT FOR FAMILY...

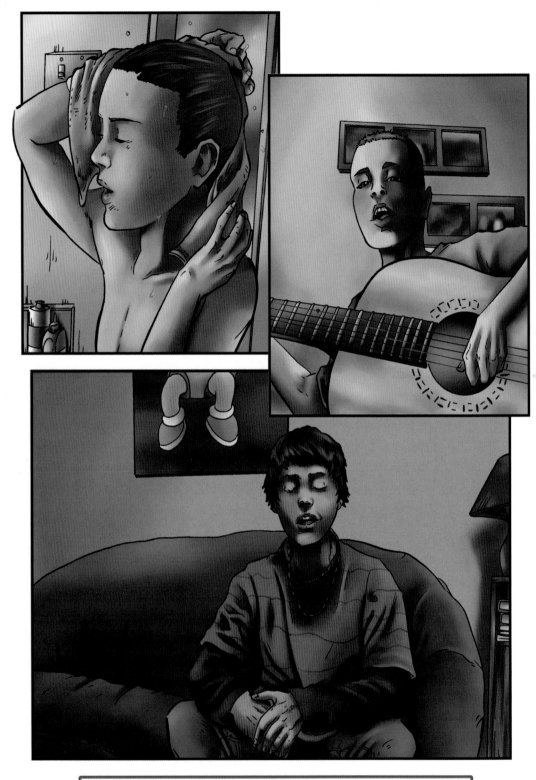

...BUT IT WASN'T LONG BEFORE THE WORLD TOOK NOTICE. IN 2007, JUSTIN BECAME A *YOU TUBE* SENSATION COVERING ARTISTS SUCH AS ALICIA KEYS, EDWIN MCCAIN, USHER, NE-YO AND CHRIS BROWN AT REQUEST FOR HIS FANS. IT DIDN'T TAKE LONG BEFORE JUSTIN'S VIDEOS REACHED OVER *10 MILLION VIEWS*.

AFTER 7 MONTHS OF **ONLINE** PERFORMANCES, FORMER **SO-SO DEF** MARKETING EXECUTIVE SCOOTER BRAUN ACCIDENTALLY CLICKED ONE OF JUSTIN'S **YOU TUBE** VIDEOS AND WAS DETERMINED TO MEET THE YOUNG PERFORMER.

BRAUN CONVINCED JUSTIN'S VERY **PROTECTIVE** MOTHER TO FLY INTO ATLANTA, GEORGIA FOR A MEETING.

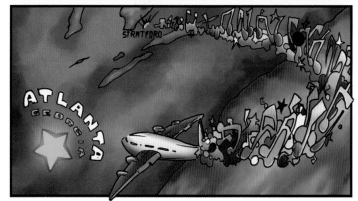

IT WAS HERE THAT A 13-YEAR-OLD JUSTIN MET **USHER** FOR THE FIRST TIME.

BUT THE MUSIC CAREER HE WAS BORN TO DIDN'T TAKE OFF RIGHT AWAY. A WEEK LATER, JUSTIN AND HIS MOTHER FLEW TO ATLANTA FOR A SECOND MEETING WITH USHER.

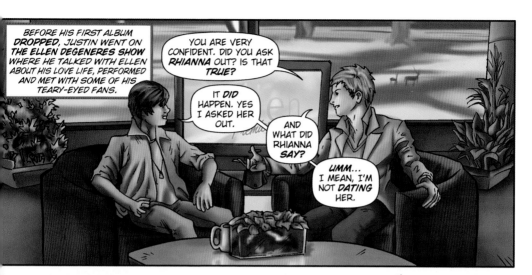

BEFORE HIS FIRST ALBUM *DROPPED*, JUSTIN WENT ON *THE ELLEN DEGENERES SHOW* WHERE HE TALKED WITH ELLEN ABOUT HIS LOVE LIFE, PERFORMED AND MET WITH SOME OF HIS TEARY-EYED FANS.

YOU ARE VERY CONFIDENT. DID YOU ASK *RHIANNA* OUT? IS THAT *TRUE?*

IT *DID* HAPPEN. YES I ASKED HER OUT.

AND WHAT DID RHIANNA *SAY?*

UMM... I MEAN, I'M NOT *DATING* HER.

AFTER THE WILD SUCCESS OF "MY WORLD," IN DECEMBER OF 2009, JUSTIN HAD THE OPPORTUNITY TO PERFORM STEVIE WONDER'S "SOMEDAY AT CHRISTMAS" FOR PRESIDENT OBAMA AND FIRST LADY AT THE WHITE HOUSE FOR CHRISTMAS IN WASHINGTON, DESPITE 'BREAKING A LEG' IN LONDON WHILE OPENING FOR TAYLOR SWIFT.

REGARDLESS OF THE FRACTURED FOOT, JUSTIN WENT TO NEW YORK TO RING IN A ROCKIN' NEW YEAR BY PERFORMING ON DICK CLARK'S ROCKIN' NEW YEAR'S EVE SPECIAL WITH RYAN SEACREST.

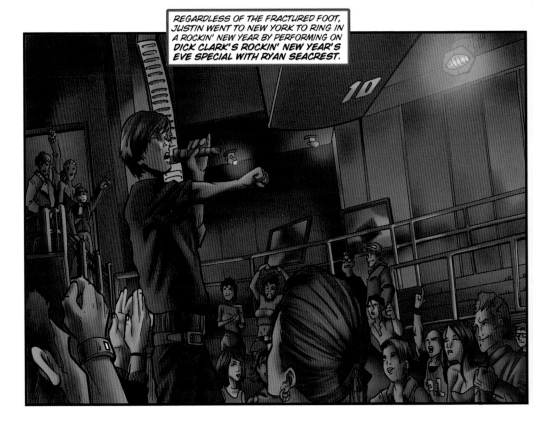

AND AT THE END OF THE DAY, JUSTIN IS YOUR AVERAGE TEEN WITH THE SAME DREAMS, FRIENDS, AND FAMILY WE ALL HAVE.

KEEPING IT HUMBLE IS SOMETHING JUSTIN STRIVES TO DO. HE KEEPS HIS FRIENDS CLOSE AND REGULARLY HEADS HOME TO STRATFORD TO SPEND TIME WITH THEM, ESPECIALLY HIS BEST BUD RYAN BUTLER. BIEBER IS ALSO A SELF-PROCLAIMED "MOMMA'S BOY," AND ON OCCASION, HE STILL GETS GROUNDED.

ON MARCH 1ST, 2010, JUSTIN TURNED 16. HE CELEBRATED BY PARTYING IN LA WITH FRIENDS AND SEEING AN **L.A. LAKERS** GAME WHERE HE MET **KOBE BRYANT**. THEN IT WAS BACK TO TORONTO FOR A CELEBRATION WITH HIS FAMILY, A LITTLE CAKE, SOME BOWLING...

...AND A NEW **RANGE ROVER** WHICH HIS MENTOR, USHER, HELPED HIM BUY. BUT THE CELEBRATION **DIDN'T** STOP THERE. AFTER RIDING AROUND IN HIS NEW WHEELS...

...HE GOT A TATTOO! JUSTIN RETURNED TO HIS HOMETOWN OF **STRATFORD**, WHERE A FRIEND OF JUSTIN'S FATHER GAVE HIM HIS FIRST **INK**. THE SEAGULL TATTOO ON HIS LEFT HIP IS RUMORED TO BE A FAMILY TRADITION.

ON MARCH 22ND, THE SECOND HALF OF HIS DEBUT ALBUM HIT STORES. IN **MY WORLD 2.0**, WE HEAR JUSTIN SING ABOUT BEING IN LOVE FOR THE FIRST TIME AND ENJOYING YOUTH.

HE EVEN PENNED THE SONG **U SMILE** FOR HIS FANS. THE ALBUM IS FULL OF SURPRISE GUESTS: LUDACRIS RAPS WITH JUSTIN ABOUT HIS FIRST LOVE IN **BABY**, JESSICA JARRELL HELPS JUSTIN GO **OVERBOARD** AND THE DUET OF SEAN KINGSTON AND BIEBER TELL HER TO MAKE UP HER MIND IN THE REGGAE INSPIRED "**EENIE MEENIE**."

ON APRIL 26, POLICE IN SYDNEY, AUSTRALIA, **CANCELED** ONE OF JUSTIN'S EVENTS DUE TO UNRULY FANS.

TWO DAYS LATER IN AUCKLAND, NEW ZEALAND, AN OVERZEALOUS GROUP OF FANS, OR "**BELIEBERS**" AS THEY ARE SOMETIMES KNOWN, WOULD RUSH JUSTIN AT THE AIRPORT KNOCKING DOWN HIS MOTHER AND STEALING HIS HAT IN THE PROCESS.

THESE INCIDENTS WOULDN'T BE THE FIRST CASES OF BIEBERMANIA'S CHAOS. IN NOVEMBER OF 2009, FANS AT A LONG ISLAND MALL IN NEW YORK GOT SO OUT OF HAND THAT AN ALBUM SIGNING WAS CALLED OFF.

AFTER THE AUCKLAND INCIDENT, JUSTIN TWEETED A GENTLE WARNING TO HIS FANS BY TELLING THEM THAT SAFETY SHOULD ALWAYS COME FIRST AT HIS EVENTS. HIS MOTHER HAD NOT BEEN HARMED AND BIEBER DIDN'T SEE A NEED TO FILE CHARGES FOR HIS STOLEN HAT SINCE IT DID GET RETURNED.

DESPITE THESE SETBACKS, JUSTIN MADE THE MOST OUT OF HIS TRIP BY VISITING A LOCAL NEWS STATION, PERFORMING A PRIVATE CONCERT AT A SCHOOL AND BUNGEE JUMPING OFF THE AUCKLAND HARBOUR BRIDGE, WHICH HE TWEETED ABOUT LATER THAT EVENING.

BUNGY! I **LOVE** NEW ZEALAND!

DESPITE HIS GOOD LOOKS AND HIS REPUTATION AS A PRANKSTER, JUSTIN TAKES HIS MUSICIANSHIP VERY SERIOUSLY.

TO PREPARE FOR HIS 2010 SUMMER TOUR, JUSTIN INSISTED THAT HE SIT IN ON THE AUDITIONS FOR HIS DANCERS AND TOURING BAND.

ONE MONTH BEFORE HEADING OUT ON TOUR, JUSTIN PRACTICES WITH HIS NEWLY AUDITIONED BAND, PERFECTS HIS DANCE MOVES AND WORKS ON HIS VOCALS.

BUT AS JUSTIN PREPARES FOR HIS UPCOMING TOUR, NO ONE KNOWS QUITE WHAT TO EXPECT. THERE IS THE PROMISE OF MEET AND GREETS BEFORE AND AFTER SHOWS, GREAT DANCING AND A FIERCE DRUMMER, SINCE JUSTIN LOVES THE DRUMS.

AT 16, JUSTIN BIEBER HAS SUNG TO SUPPORT THE VICTIMS OF THE HAITIAN EARTHQUAKE WITH "WE ARE THE WORLD - 25 FOR HAITI," AND HE HAS MINGLED WITH SUPERSTARS AND APPEARED ON COUNTLESS TELEVISION PROGRAMS IN ADDITION TO TOPPING MUSIC CHARTS WORLDWIDE, BUT WHAT'S NEXT FOR THE KID FROM CANADA WHO HAS WON OVER THE HEARTS OF TWEENS AND TEENS ACROSS THE GLOBE?